First published in Great Britain in 2014 by Greenbird Books

©2014 Malak Afaneh

Text copyright Malak Afaneh

Illustrations copyright Tashna Salim

This book has been typeset in DaunPenh

Printed in USA

British Library Cataloguing in Publication Data:

A catalogue record for this book is available from the

British Library.

ISBN 978-0-9576379-8-6

www.greenbirdbooks.com

To my little sister Amal...

nour (light) of inspiration.

The smell of exotic spices and the shouting of children signalled the start of a busy Friday in Damascus, Syria. Skipping across the street merrily, Nour widened her eyes and gazed at the unfamiliar sights surrounding her. Rows of bazaars and stalls were lined up, filled to the brim with spices, fruit, veggies, baked goods, hummus, falafel, and sweets. Tightening her hold on her mother's hand, Nour inspected the goods curiously, comparing them to the ones back at home in America. Suddenly, she saw a pair of warm, brown eyes staring at her. She jumped back, frightened, and hid behind her mother.

In front of her stood a middle aged man with kind eyes and a warm smile, who she knew. He owned many of the bazaars in the market.

"Did I frighten you?" asked the man. He took one of the large apples and handed it to her.

"Why don't you take an apple on your way?"

Nour slowly took the apple from him, and thanked him for his kindness. She enjoyed the rare feeling of belonging in a Middle-Eastern community, where the residents helped out one another by offering food and gifts, sewing clothes for the children, and providing for others who didn't have as much money.

As Nour bit into the apple and continued by her mother's side, she noticed her neighbor, Ayesha, playing soccer with the other children, using an old, worn-out cloth soccer ball.

"*Marhaba*, Nour!" called Ayesha, greeting her in Arabic. "Would you like to play?"

"Sorry, Ayesha, I can't. I would get my new prayer clothes dirty," said Nour, making sure to show all the children her wonderful prayer clothes.

Ayesha stared at them and said, "Wow Nour! Those are really cute prayer clothes! I'm going to tell my mom to get me some like those!" She then left and returned to her game.

Nour smiled broadly as she straightened out her prayer clothes. Her grandfather, her *seedo*, as she called him in Arabic, had gotten these for her as a welcoming gift. She thought back to that warm afternoon with *Seedo* praying on his rosary beads.

They were made of marble, with a cherry red color and silver string holding them together. Nour had stared at them continuously. Whilst she watched, her grandfather took a green box, covered in red silk ribbon from under the couch and placed it on her lap.

Excited, Nour opened the box with trembling fingers and found a string of rosary beads. They were made of beautiful purple crystals, shining in the light, casting shadows of purple across the room.

"Look at your second gift, Nour," said *seedo*.

Nour looked more closely in the box, and found a brand new set of prayer clothes, just like the ones the other girls in the neighborhood owned. There were two pieces, a long head covering to the waist, and a skirt to match. Nour fingered the soft white fabric, which was covered in delicate green flowers, with a lace edge.

"I heard your mother is going this Friday for the prayers, maybe you could ask to go with her!" smiled *seedo*.

Nour smiled. She was so busy remembering how pleased she had been to receive those gifts that she didn't notice that they had already reached the door of the masjid.

She gazed up, wonderstruck at the beauty of the intricate designs covering the masjid's walls. Delicate calligraphy bordered the edge of wall with carefully hand drawn crescents to match, all the way to the dome of the masque. The room was bare, with green carpet, and a few bookshelves where the Holy Book, the Quran, was kept.

Nour was thrilled to enter the masjid for the first time, she walked to the prayer rugs and sat down, clutching her rosary beads tightly, feeling the marble in her hand as she counted.

Suddenly, a tall man with a dark beard and a long white robe appeared, approaching Nour and her mother. She clutched her mother's skirt, and drew close behind her. Nour recognized the man to be an Imam, the leader of the masjid.

"I'm very sorry sister, but you can't be here," he gently said, addressing Nour's mom. "We have too many men to accommodate the women for Friday Prayers."

Nour was worried. Did this mean she wouldn't get the chance to pray in her new prayer clothes?

Nour's mom looked surprised. "I'm very sorry, Imam, but we are visitors from America, and it is our first time in this area. Is there any way we could stay just this time?"

The Imam shook his head. "I'm sorry, but that won't be possible. We simply have no room."

Nour's mom took her hand, and led her calmly out of the masjid. Her mom looked at her sadly and explained that they would have to try another masjid farther away. Nour nodded her head, holding back her tears, and trying to hide how upset she was.

After ten minutes, Nour and her mom reached the door of the second masjid, which looked very similar to the first one. They opened the door quietly, embracing the cool air compared to the sweltering heat outside.

Another Imam again apologized to them, the masjid also had no room for women for Friday prayers.

"Please, Imam, is there any way we can go to pray? It's my daughters first time going to the Friday prayers, and she is so excited to experience praying in a group!" exclaimed Nour's mom, pleading.

The Imam looked at Nour thoughtfully. "You could try Umayyad Masjid in Old Damascus. They have plenty of room there for women."

Nour felt a spark of hope as she heard the news. If they hurried, she could go and pray like a big girl and get to use her prayer clothes and her colorful rosary beads! Nour's mom walked out, after thanking the Imam.

Nour and her mom walked through Al-Hamidiyya market, an old covered market leading to the Umayyad Masjid. Nour was thrilled to see bustling antique shops, different vendors offering Arabic coffee, Tamarind and mulberry drinks, sweets, tradional clothing and gifts.

"Why did we have to leave those other masjids! It was not fair mommy!" exclaimed Nour, glancing at the shops.

Nour's mother patted her back, comforting her. "Unfortunately, Nour, many masjids in this area are not used to having women arrive for Friday prayers. Also, it seems a lot more men show up, so masjids have started letting the men pray in the women's prayer rooms."

Nour widened her eyes, shocked. "B-But...Mom! It's the women's prayer room, only they should be allowed to use it!"

"What do you think we should do?" asked Nour's mom.

"Maybe we can tell the Imam to keep a space for women," suggested Nour.

"That's a great idea," said Nour's mom.

"Or we could ask Aunty Fatima and her friends to come with us too," added Nour.

"Mom, does Allah say that women can't go to the Friday Prayers?"

Nour's mom crouched down till she was face to face with her daughter. "No, darling, Allah doesn't say that. Allah says that women should not be forbidden from going to masjids. Allah also encourages all to go to Friday prayers, not only men but also women and children if they like to."

Nour and her mom arrived just on time to the Umayyad Masjid. The masjid was big with golden wall designs.

Many children were running around the open courtyard, excitedly racing between slender columns while hundreds of pigeons were hovering over domes and arches.

Nour could see there were many spaces to pray and she ran ahead to find a prayer mat. After the prayers, Nour smiled at her mother and said, "Thanks, Mom. Can we go show *seedo* how I look with the prayer clothes on?"

Nour's mom laughed. "Didn't you show him this morning?"

"Well..Yes. But can I still show him again?"

"Of course, honey! Let's go home then!"

Nour grabbed her mom's hand again, and started skipping home, passing the bazaar. Ayesha was still playing soccer, and shop owners had just gotten back from the Friday prayers also. She ran all the way, through streets and alleys, untill she arrived, breathless, at the front door of her house.

She pushed the front door open, finding her *seedo* sitting on the couch, using his rosary beads, having arrived from the prayers.

"*Seedo!*" shouted Nour, excited to tell him about her day.

Seedo smiled, his eyes twinkling, as he kissed Nour. "How was your day?"

Nour jumped on the couch eagerly, and put her hand

on his arm. "Well, they didn't have enough room at the local masjids, so we went to the Umayyad Masjid. It was lots of fun. I felt a bit upset in the beginning, but Mom said when I get to be a really big girl, things will be better in all the masjids!"

Seedo smiled and said, "Yes Nour, you learned a very important lesson about patience today. Allah rewards all those who never give up to do good. And you my child are full of goodness!"

Nour smiled and looked at her grandfather, "Well I guess I must get that from you then, my lovely *seedo*!"

Both Nour and her grandfather laughed, as the sun finally set on that beautiful Friday evening.

Also by Malak Afaneh, availale to buy
from Amazon US, UK & EU

www.greenbirdbooks.com

28819915R10018

Made in the USA
Charleston, SC
23 April 2014